SUVARNABHUMI AIRPORT

Bangkok, Thailand

Helmut Jahn
Werner Sobek
Matthias Schuler

avedition

Imprint

Bibliographic information published by Die Deutsche Nationalbibliothek.
Die Deutsche Nationalbibliothek lists this publication in the Deutsche
Nationalbibliografie; detailed bibliographic data is available on the Internet at
http://dnb.d-nb.de.

Design	Jason Pickleman, Keith Palmer, and Tracy Erski
Photography	Rainer Viertlböck
Prepress	L&N Litho, Waiblingen
Production	atio_druckkonzepte, Leinfelden-Echterdingen
Printed by	Dr. Cantz'sche Druckerei, Ostfildern
Paper	150 gsm 'Galaxy Keramik'

© 2007 avedition GmbH, Ludwigsburg
Publishers for Architecture and Design
Koenigsallee 57, D – 71638 Ludwigsburg
contact@avedition.com, www.avedition.com
© 2007 the authors and copyright holders for texts and plans
© 2007 Rainer Viertlböck for the photographs

ISBN 978-3-89986-088-7

Printed in Germany
Prepress and printing: 'Aniva'® 4 color process system

SUVARNABHUMI AIRPORT

Bangkok, Thailand

Airports of Thailand	Owner
Murphy / Jahn	Architect
ACT Consultants	Associate Architect / Engineer
TAMS Consultants / Earth Tech	Project Management
Werner Sobek Ingenieure	Structural Concept / Concourse Superstructure / Facades
Transsolar Energietechnik	Climate and Environmental Concept
Martin / Martin	Main Terminal Superstructure
John A. Martin & Associates	Structural Concrete
Flack + Kurtz	Mechanical / Electrical / Plumbing
Blum Laboratorium	Acoustical Consultant
Yann Kersalé	Lighting Art
NT Architects-Planners	Interior Artwork
BNP Associates, Inc.	Baggage Consultant
ITO Joint Venture	General Contractor
Italian-Thai Development	
Takenaka Corporation	
Obayashi Corporation	

The passenger terminal complex at Suvarnabhumi Airport resulted from an international competition and established the basis of collaboration between Helmut Jahn, Werner Sobek, and Matthias Schuler.

Suvarnabhumi Airport best represents the goal to construct buildings where nothing must be added and nothing can be taken away.
The Airport's identity will become associated with Bangkok and Thailand and be considered one of its new 'Icons.'

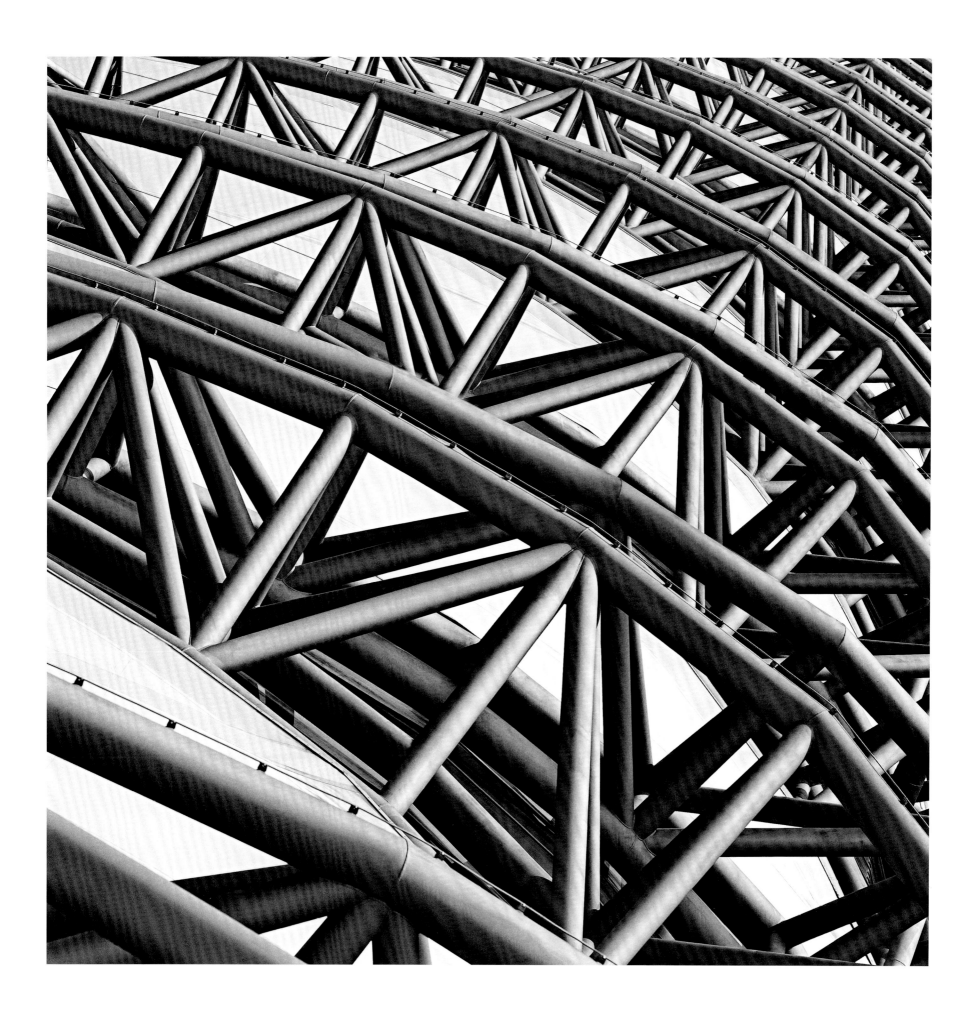

Passenger Terminal Complex Suvarnabhumi International Airport Bangkok, Thailand

Helmut Jahn

The passenger terminal complex at Suvarnabhumi Airport resulted from an International Competition and established the basis of collaboration between Werner Sobek, Matthias Schuler, and Helmut Jahn. The challenge was great and unusual. The task of creating a new gateway to Thailand in a tropical climate necessitated a different approach to architecture and engineering. Through the integration of the disciplines the complex problem resulted in a sophisticated, intelligent yet simple solution. After 11 years of planning and construction the Terminal opened for passenger traffic in late 2006.

The design took into consideration Murphy/Jahn's experience with airport terminal design, starting in the 1950's. Those buildings included *O'Hare International Airport in Chicago* and particularly the *New United Airlines Terminal* of the mid-1980's and the near completed renovation of *Terminal 3* for *American Airlines* and *Terminal 2*; the work in the commercial zone of the New Munich Airport, which included the *Kempinski Hotel*, the *Munich Airport Center* and infrastructure, parking and landscaped areas; and the new *Terminal 2* and the *Train-Station* at the Airport in *Cologne/Bonn*.

It also responded to the challenge that airports today are a *New Building Type*. They have become a strange combination of Transportation Center and 'Mall.' They constitute cities outside cities and give the first and last impression of a city, region, or country. They are places to meet for people of all facets of life.

Architecturally important to us is the openness, comprehension and experience of the open spaces, the gesture of the roof as a memorable image, and the way the blurring of the boundaries between public and private space make an airport terminal a model of a *'Mini-City.'* Like in a city the experience leads through squares, streets, and rooms for transportation, commerce and private uses.

In our practice we have been interested since the early 1990's in the integration of technology and design, with the goal of designing buildings with a totally integrated approach, breaking down the barriers that often exist between Architecture and Engineering, which we refer to as *Archi-Neering*.

In the design and execution of Suvarnabhumi Airport, innovative and integrated architectural, structural and environmental design were used, new materials and systems of advanced technology were developed, and unusual construction processes required to meet the design goals. The goal was to strive for transparency and elevate systems and materials in their construction to a level of art.

The results are advanced long span, lightweight steel structures, exposed pre-cast concrete structures, clear or low e-coated glass, a three-layer translucent membrane, integrated cooling, using water as a low energy carrier and the thermal mass of concrete and a displacement ventilation system with minimal air changes.

Those components and parts serve in their total composition and in use more than in their conventional roles. They maximize daylight and comfort, yet minimize the use of energy with significant life cycle cost savings. The installed cooling power is reduced close to 50% compared to a conventional system. The three-layer translucent membrane was developed to mediate between the exterior and interior conditions, dealing with heat and noise transmission, while still allowing for natural daylight within the building.

The result is a building flooded with controlled daylight in a tropical climate. Architect and Engineer speak the same language. This starts often with finding a concept for a building together and carries through the design and workings of a building's structure, energy/comfort systems and enclosure. Systems and components are not looked upon as separate, but as integral building parts. For instance, the enclosure, which includes both facade and roof, is considered a component, which modulates the climate of a building and deals with daylight, natural ventilation, solar energy and their interaction with the buildings' technical systems. In the process, the team works with specialists in the field of glass, fabrics, plastics, coatings, aerodynamics, and components, which heat and cool buildings and are often integrated with structure, facade, floor, or ceiling.

The point is that the architect thinks more about the technical consequences of the forms he designs and the engineers have to consider the aesthetic results of their concepts and decisions.

Suvarnabhumi Airport best represents the goal to construct buildings where nothing must be added and nothing can be taken away.

In a building with such an advanced technical concept and construct it is important to establish a connection to local cultural tradition and art. This is done through the shaded gardens flanking the terminal, which represent Thai landscape in cities and in the country, a jungle garden between the terminal and concourse, traditional artistic patterns and colors on glazed surfaces and floors, and Thai artifacts placed at the airside centers and concourses. From departure to arrival there is a succession of varying experiences in space and light. This gives clear *Orientation* to the users, should reduce the anxiety associated with travel and be full of *Delight*. Its *Identity* will become associated with Bangkok and Thailand and be considered one of its new 'Icons.'

This makes Suvarnabhumi Airport Thailand's own *Gateway to the World*. •

The Structural Concept

Werner Sobek

A building flooded with natural light, a building which—beyond all the complex functions an airport has to fulfill—provides openness and easy orientation requires structural systems which combine structural logic, consequent reduction of deadweight, and perfection down to the least detail. Suvarnabhumi International Airport with its large spaces to cover, the necessity to reduce the need of energy and material to the minimum, and the exposure of the structural system, which at this time became an important part of the architectural appearance, required on the one side a hand-in-glove approach of the architect, the structural, the facade, and the energy engineers, which we call Archi-Neering, and on the other side pushed structural engineers to new limits.

The roof of the terminal buildings is an excellent example for the integration of structural consequence and architectural intention. Having overall dimensions in plan of 570m x 210m, the roof is supported by 16 columns only. Main girders connect two columns each, bridging a clear span of 126m and cantilevering at each of their ends by another 42m. The main girder spacing is 81m, which compares to a bridge of noteworthy span. Both main and secondary girders have been designed as steel trusses being as light as possible. In addition, the main girders, because of the huge loads they have to carry, have been shaped expressively but structurally consequent by adjusting the structural height to their moment-diagram. The three chords of the main girders have been arranged with two chords where compression forces have to be transferred but one chord where the tension forces are to be taken. Whereas the top chord of the truss is composed of two chords at midspan, the girders show one top chord only at their support, which are the columns. Hence, the cross section of the girder varies

along its axis, not only in height but also in its configuration, thus yielding to a structural element which embodies both structural logic and architectural quality. The same design philosophy is also met at the facade of the terminal buildings, which is one of the largest glazed areas found today and which, again, embodies consequent lightweight engineering and a consequent architectural approach. The facade, which is about 1,100m long in plan and 30m high, is supported by underslung vertical steel pipes acting as posts, each of them 25m high. The posts are connected by prestressed cable trusses that are also connected to the 2.25 x 2.25m glass panes forming the skin of the terminal. At the end, the facade, with its huge dimensions, looks simple in its structure and detail and laymen often wonder how such little material can withstand such huge wind forces as occur in Thailand. However, it is nothing but consequent and sound engineering that makes such solutions possible. The search for simplicity, a minimized amount of material to be installed, and rigorous consequence in all of the decisions a structural engineer has to make were the driving forces while we were designing this facade, a situation we faced in the same way while designing the loadbearing structures for the concourse roofs. These, covering the concourses with a clear span of 42m and with a total length of 3,200m, are formed by five-hinge arch-type structures with exposed steel trusses. Structural fabric and glazed steel grid shells span from truss to truss, establishing a sound and thermal proof enclosure which is nothing but a structure, a building skin, and an outstanding piece of architecture, all in one. •

Innovative Climate Concept

Matthias Schuler

The purpose of climate engineering for buildings is to ensure the highest possible comfort for occupants with the lowest possible impact on the environment. Transsolar worked collaboratively with the architects, structural engineers, mechanical engineers, and other consultants from the start of the building design process, considering each step from the standpoint of fundamental thermodynamics and physics. This generates a climate concept in which local conditions, form, material, and mechanical systems are synergistic components of a well-orchestrated climate control system.

THE TERMINAL'S ENVELOPE

Conditioning a building with respect to an ensured user comfort and a limited energy consumption has become an integral component of building design. Bangkok's climate is characterized by temperatures between 25°C and 30°C, with a high level of relative humidity and solar radiation, and with solar altitudes near the zenith. An international airport—with heat loads emitted by people, electric equipment, and lighting—requiring a constant air temperature (24°C) and 50%–60% relative humidity calls for continual cooling and dehumidification. These specifications place high demands on the building envelope to minimize the effects of solar loads. The sheds in the terminal (measuring 570m x 210m) use fritted single-pane glass with 95% opacity on the north side, and solid panels limiting the solar gain to 1% of the radiation striking the south side. A cantilevered, louvered roof shades the 30m-high vertical glazing.

FLOOR COOLING AND DISPLACEMENT VENTILATION

Air-conditioning of large-volume enclosures with internal building elements requires a great amount of energy; conventional systems are uneconomical in light of the ratio of volume to area in use. By partitioning the building in zones of unconditioned spaces and cooled occupied zones, the total cooling demand is drastically reduced because air-conditioning is only administered where needed. Two different cooling systems are used. First, there is radiant floor cooling directly removing radiation striking the floor. The floor stays cool, increasing thermal comfort. The second system is an air displacement system, with a controllable air stream supplying cool air to the space at floor level and at low velocity. In addition to using a portion of return air for the rejection of convection heat loads, the system provides the required cooled and dehumidified fresh air to the space.

THERMAL AIR STRATIFICATION

Because cool air is heavier than warm air, thermal stratification is induced in the building, supported by the radiant floor cooling (FIG.1). The zone which is air-conditioned extends only 2.5m above floor level. In the unconditioned higher levels the air is approximately ambient temperature; therefore it is not necessary to insulate this part of the envelope. Due to the thermal air stratification, this has no influence on the conditioned, inhabited spaces below.

INNOVATIVE THREE-LAYER MEMBRANE ROOF

In the concourses the same cooling principle was applied, but here the circumstances are different. Transparent glazing and translucent panels alternate in the building envelope. In order to meet the requirements for high transparency and solar protection against low-latitude sun, the degree to which the glass panels are fritted increases toward the roof. The membrane roof also had to fulfil a number of requirements. It must admit 1%–2% of the sunlight, as diffuse light, in order to provide the basic ambient lighting (FIG. 2); it may not, however, permit additional solar radiation to enter, in order to limit the energy gain in the space in use (FIG. 3). In addition, the heat radiation from the hot roof must be reduced to approximately 40% in order to meet the energy consumption limitations for the space. For sound protection countering exterior noises (aircraft noise) a sound reduction index of 35dB is required, and for favorable acoustics there is a 60% absorption rate toward the interior. The newly developed membrane package consists of an outer membrane of Teflon-coated glass fibers, a coated inner membrane level, and transparent PC sheets on a steel-cable mesh. The inner membrane—translucent as a result of miniscule perforation—serves,

Fig. 1: Temperature stratification
        in the concourse section

Fig. 2: 'Waiting in the light' daylight
        evaluation for the hold
        rooms at the gates

Fig. 3: Concourse energy and
        comfort concept

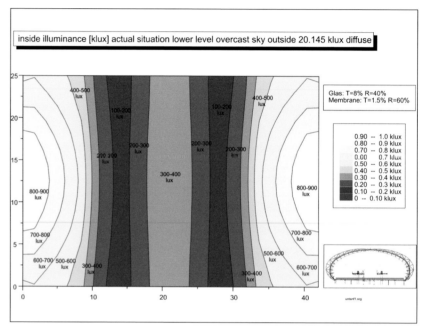

inside illuminance [klux] actual situation lower level overcast sky outside 20.145 klux diffuse

Glas: T=8% R=40%
Membrane: T=1.5% R=60%

0.90 -- 1.0 klux
0.80 -- 0.9 klux
0.70 -- 0.8 klux
0.00 -- 0.7 klux
0.50 -- 0.6 klux
0.40 -- 0.5 klux
0.30 -- 0.4 klux
0.20 -- 0.3 klux
0.10 -- 0.2 klux
0 -- 0.10 klux

Fig. 2

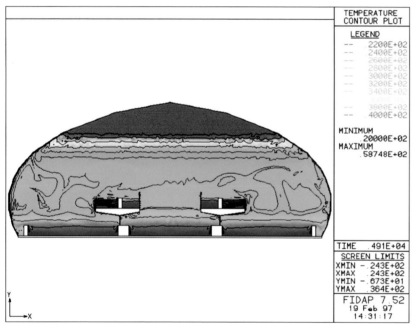

Fig. 1

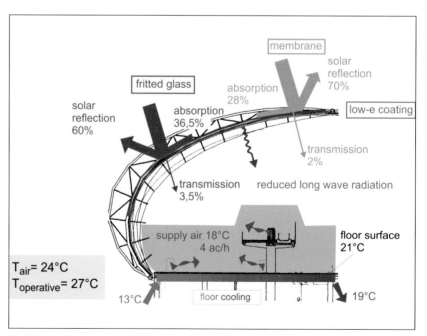

Fig. 3

in conjunction with the PC sheets, as a baffle. The coating on the side facing the interior has low-emissivity characteristics (low-e). Low-e coatings block the radiative heat exchange between the warm membrane and the inhabited spaces. This characteristic of the inner surface has an additional advantage: instead of permitting the heat from the roof to pass through it, it reflects the 'cool' thermal radiation which is then reflected by a thermal mirror into the room, improving, in conjunction with the floor cooling, the occupants' thermal comfort.

SIMULATION AND MEASUREMENT

The verification for the energy and ventilation concept was attained by means of sophisticated simulations. The building's thermal stratification as well as the conveyance of humidity was examined in stationary and transient fluid dynamic simulations (CFD). A decisive step in demonstrating, prior to construction, how the concept works was the experimental verification of the stable thermal stratification. At the scale 1:3 temperatures and indoor air movement were measured in a tennis hall with a translucent membrane roof and an air-conditioning system comparable to the one proposed for the concourse segments. Under hot summer conditions the nascent thermal stratification's stability was visualized with the assistance of smoke injections. The boundary layer was shown to be stable, despite a temperature gradient that was smaller than under actual conditions, and was not disturbed by the ventilation system or by occupants.

In the laboratory and *in situ* measurements the material parameters of the building envelope were checked with respect to the energy consumption specified in the optimized building concept in order to achieve the thermal comfort with the appropriately dimensioned cooling and ventilation systems. A 1:1 mockup of a concourse bay on site with the low-e membrane and the floor cooling proved the previous tests.

ENERGY AND CO_2 CONSERVATION

The comparison of the building envelope and air–conditioning concept specifically developed and realized for this project to a standard reference system showed savings in the energy consumption of 35%, which correspond to CO_2 savings of around 65,000 tons every year. •

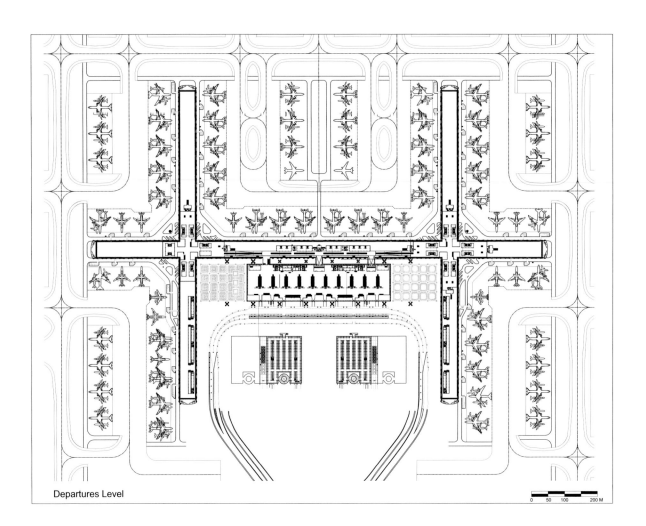

Departures Level

0   50   100   200 M

The Airport itself becomes the first and last impression of a City/Region or Country. A 'city outside cities,' airports have become a new building type combining transportation services and the conveniences of a mall-centered culture.

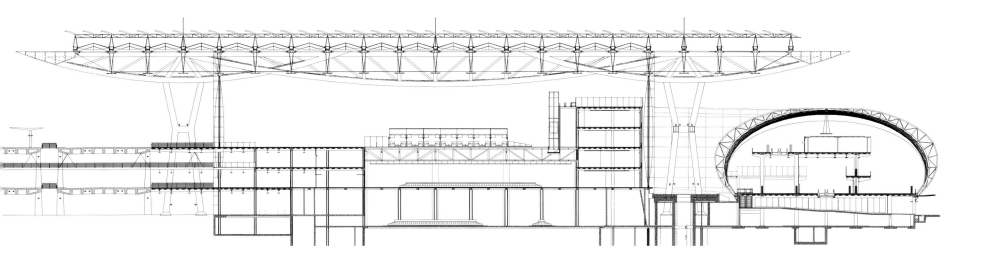

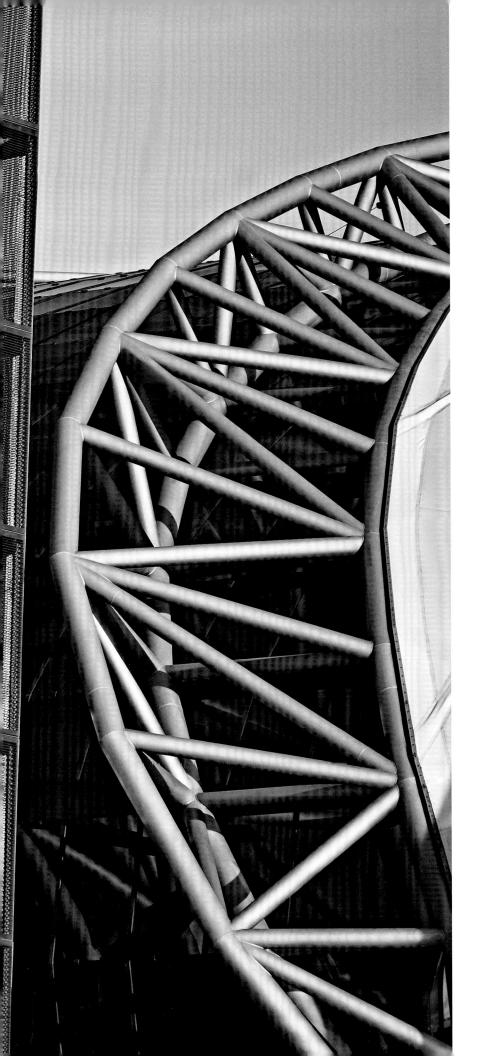

Systems and components are not looked upon as separate, but integral parts.

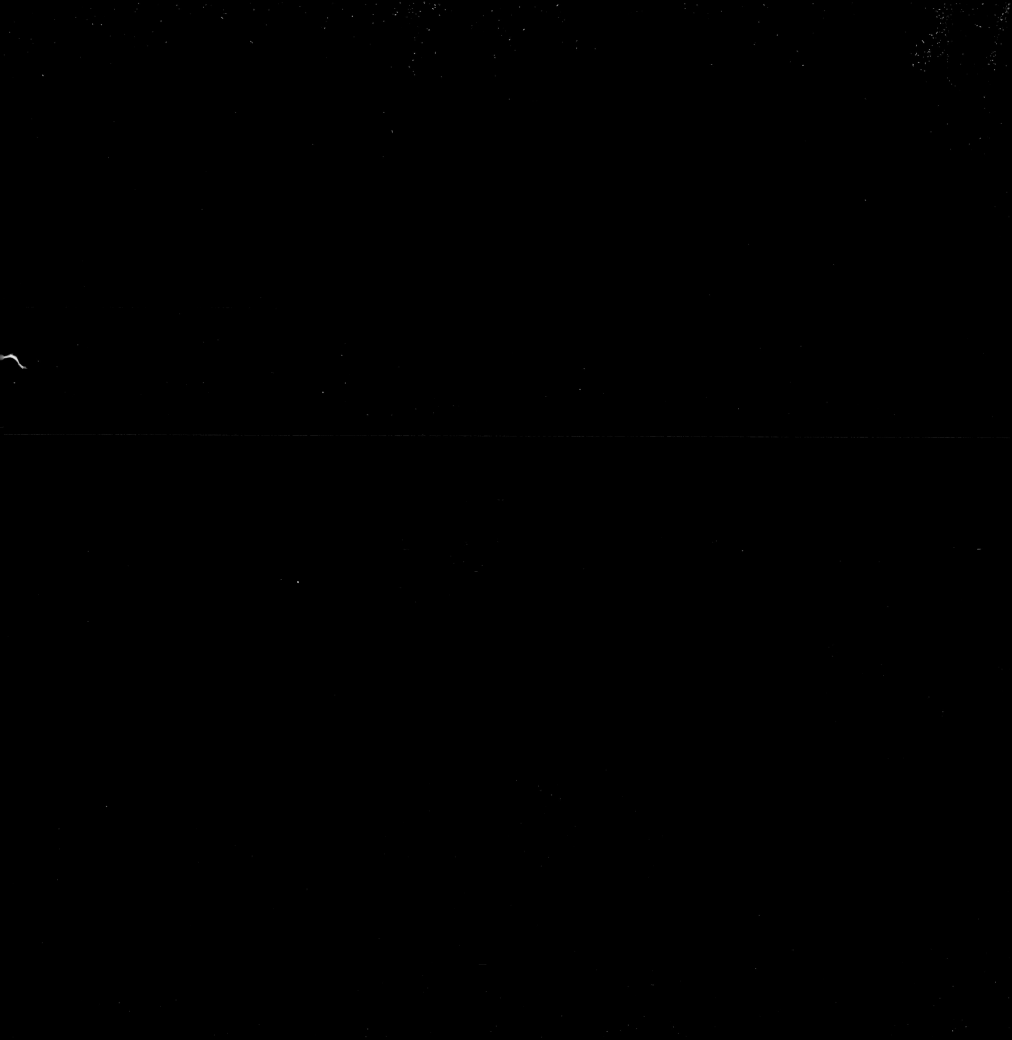

The roof rests on eight pairs of columns; each pair supporting a primary truss, which in turn supports a series of secondary trusses, which support the sun protection elements.

Open space, the gesture of the roof, and the blurring of the boundaries between public and private space make the Suvarnabhumi Airport Terminal a model of a Mini-City with squares, streets, and purposefully contained uses.

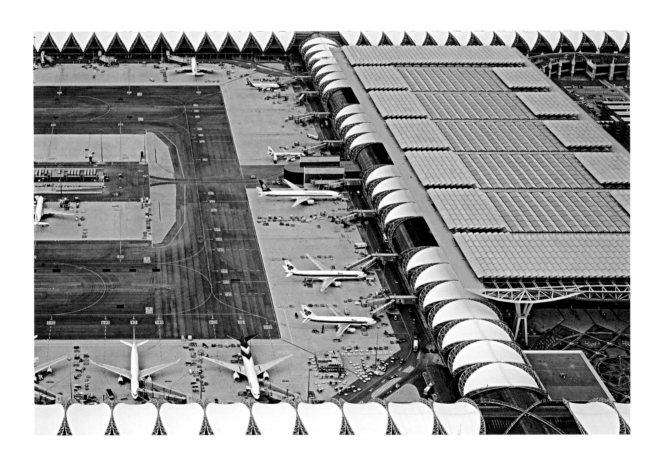

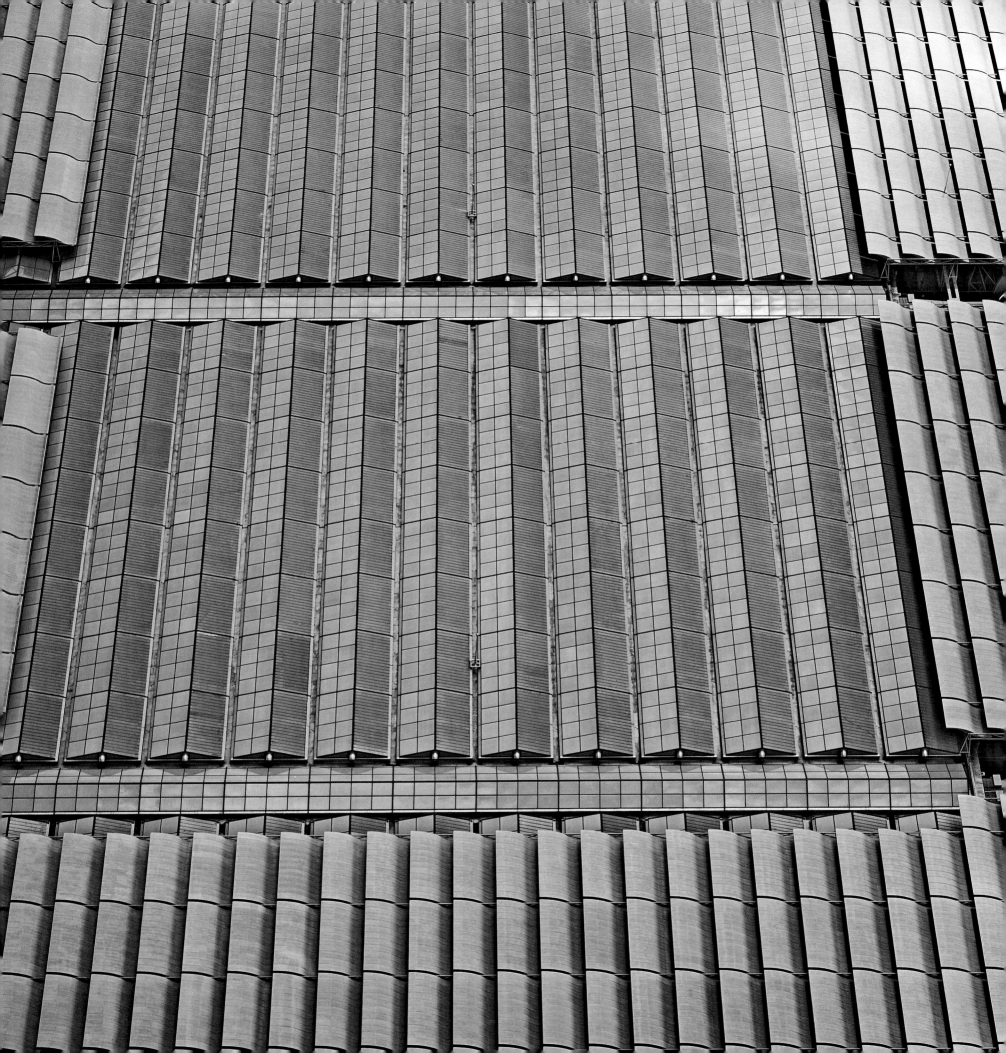

Shaded gardens flanking the terminal represent Thai landscapes as seen in the region's cities and outlaying rural areas.

A jungle garden between the terminal and concourse reflects the texture and nuance unique to Thailand.

Traditional artistic patterns and colors on glazed surfaces and floors, along with Thai artifacts, at the airside centers and concourses create visual as well as temporal markers and provide a connection to the local cultural traditions.

The three-layer translucent membrane was developed to mediate between the exterior and interior conditions, dealing with heat and noise transmission, while still allowing for natural daylight within the building.

Gate E10   Gate E1

↑ 🛂 ตรวจคนเข้าเมือง
Immigration
↑ 🧳 รับกระเป๋า Baggage Claim 16-23
→ 🧳 รับกระเป๋า Baggage Claim 6-15

Past, present, and future are seamlessly integrated, making
Suvarnabhumi Airport Thailand's own gateway to the world.

Acknowledgements

Murphy / Jahn

Helmut Jahn
Sam Scaccia
Thomas Chambers
Sanford Gorshow
Carl D'Silva
Joseph Stypka
Dan Cubric
Phil Castillo
Martin Wolf
Jaak Jürisson
Chad Mitchell
Joan Hu
J.J. Tang
T.J. McLeish
Bess Tremonto-Cook
Lawrence Malsky
Michael Castrogiovanni
Mattias Lassen
Scott Seyer
Alice Kriegel
Anja Rosenburg
Richard Drinkwater

ACT Consultants

Vanchai Vimuktayon
Montree Taranurak
Taungthong
　Anekpuritanang
Poktawee Sridama
Phamorn Suebjakdee
Sumedhard
　Udomkarnjananon
Manoon Arayasiri
Permsak Toonsakool
Surachai Chantajaru
Chatchai Bhamarasuta
Thirawat Somwadi
Sira Jirapaisankul
Pitsanu Boonyaphak
Sak Vimuktayon
Sombut Sukkal
Veerayuth Kingkeaw
Janeson Chakajnarodom
Nava Voravudthichanyakul
Visuth Shoterawong
Soontorn Wacheeworasit

TAMS / EarthTech

Ed Regan
Brian O'Connor
Lyle Hixenbaugh
George Emery
Andrew Zdzienicki
David Karlquist
Andrew Linder
David Black
Doug Schuerman
Art Fox
Mike Derin
Richard Silverstein
Jose Mandujano
Jerry Farrar
Mark Piltingsrud
Martin Conisbee
Tony O'Connor
Chris Jolly
Pakarat (Nok)
　Tungthumwong

Werner Sobek Ingenieure

Werner Sobek
Josef Linder
Viktor Wilhelm
Markus Aberle
Thanapon Buamongkol
Markus Buschmann
Berthold Eger
Gert Eilbracht
Steffen Feirabend
Eduard Ganz
Walter Haase
Wilfried Laufs
Thomas Müller
Birgit Piehl
Wolfgang Rudolph
Anvar Sadykov
Julia Stratil
Klaus Straub
Antje Sydow
Martin Synold

Transsolar
Energietechnik

Matthias Schuler
Stefan Holst
Thomas Lechner
Stefanie Reuss
Torsten Welfonder
Friedemann Kik

John A. Martin
Associates
Martin/Martin

John A. Martin
Charles Keyes
Stan Welton
Tim Lack
Laura Kannady

Flack+Kurtz

Reginald Monteyne
Wayne Gaw
Peter Simmonds
Randy J. Meyers
Pete G. Samaras
Patrick Kenny

Blum
Laboratorium

Rainer Blum

AIK Expéditions
Lumière

Yann Kersalé
Christian Arhan

NT Architects–
Planners

Trungjai
  Buranasomphob
Manoo Kupatavinij
Panya Vijinthanasarn
Manop Pakinsee

BNP

Damien Breier
Rich Linke

ITO Joint Venture

Italian-Thai Development Public Co., Ltd.
Tawatchai Suthiprapha

Takenaka Corporation
Shiro Osada

Obayashi Corporation
Masahide Kuniyoshi

Photoshooting of the airport was
carried out over a period of one
year with a shooting time of 22
weeks. In order to show connecting
structures of the building complex,
most of the external photos were
taken with the aid of a 49m-high
lifting platform. The aerial photos
were taken from a helicopter both
before and after the airport started
operating. During the long period,
it was necessary in particular to
make use of the narrow time
windows between the completion
of different building sections and
the subsequent immediate conver-
sion by the individual operators.
In order to present the interior
areas as far as possible in their
un-changed architectural intention,
entire parts of the buildings were
cleared, blocked off, and photo-
graphed. This was one of the first
architectural photoshootings to
be carried out using a special
view camera with high-resolution
22 and 33 megapixel digital backs
by Sinar.

—Rainer Viertlböck, Photographer